Little Pebble™

Transport

Ships

by Mari Schuh

raintree

a Capstone company — publishers for children

Raintree is an imprint of Capstone Global Library Limited, a company incorporated in England and Wales
having its registered office at 264 Banbury Road, Oxford, OX2 7DY – Registered company number: 6695582

www.raintree.co.uk
myorders@raintree.co.uk

Edited by Carrie Braulick Sheely
Designed by Lori Bye
Picture research by Wanda Winch
Production by Katy LaVigne
Originated by Capstone Global Library Limited
Printed and bound in India

ISBN 978 1 4747 4430 0 (hardback)
21 20 19 18 17
10 9 8 7 6 5 4 3 2 1

ISBN 978 1 4747 4436 2 (paperback)
22 21 20 19 18
10 9 8 7 6 5 4 3 2 1

British Library Cataloguing in Publication Data
A full catalogue record for this book is available from the British Library.

Acknowledgements
We would like to thank the following for permission to reproduce photographs: Dreamstime: Jordanker, 11;
Shutterstock: Alex Kolokythas Photography, 21, Alvov, 13, amophoto_au, 15, donvictorio, 7, Eastimages, 9, Igor
Karasi, 17, Ivan Cholakov, 5, Nightman1965, cover, T. Sumaetho, zoom motion design; U.S. Navy Photo by Petty
Officer 3rd Class Nathan T. Beard, 18–19

Every effort has been made to contact copyright holders of material reproduced in this book. Any omissions will
be rectified in subsequent printings if notice is given to the publisher.

All the internet addresses (URLs) given in this book were valid at the time of going to press. However, due to
the dynamic nature of the internet, some addresses may have changed, or sites may have changed or ceased to
exist since publication. While the author and publisher regret any inconvenience this may cause readers, no
responsibility for any such changes can be accepted by either the author or the publisher.

Contents

At sea

A ship sails by.

People wave.

Hello!

Parts

Look at the big engine.

It makes power.

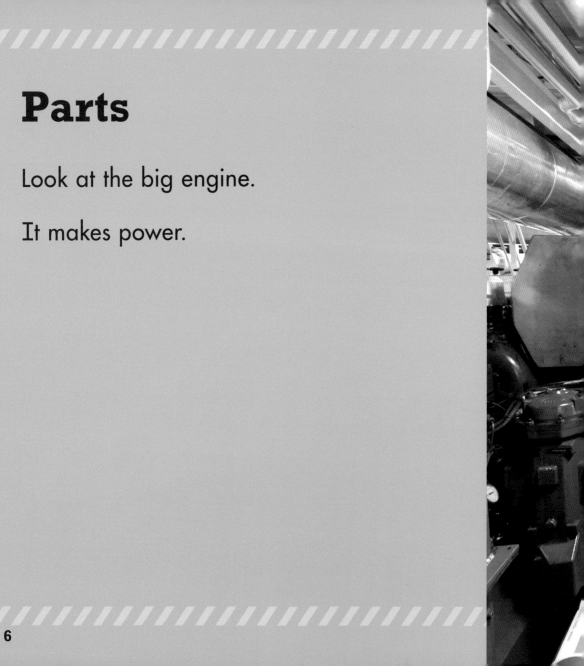

engine

Look at the propeller.

The engine makes it spin.

Then the ship moves.

propeller

Look at the rudder.

It helps to steer the ship.

rudder

This ship has sails.

Sails use the wind to move the ship.

Types

Look at the cruise ship.

It is full of people.

They have fun!

A tanker is full of liquid.

It carries tonnes of oil.

Here is an aircraft carrier.

It carries fighter planes.

Time for take-off!

Here is a cargo ship.

It carries big boxes.

What might be inside?

Glossary

aircraft carrier ship with a large, flat deck where aircraft take off and land

cargo ship ship that carries large amounts of goods

cruise ship large ship that people travel on for holidays

engine machine that makes the power needed to move something

propeller set of rotating blades that make the force to move a ship through water

rudder flat metal piece attached to a ship that is used for steering

sail large sheet of strong cloth on a ship; a sail catches the wind to move the ship

tanker ship that carries large amounts of liquid in tanks

Find out more

Books

Big Machines Float! (Big Machines), Catherine Veitch (Raintree, 2015)

Getting Around Through the Years: How Transport has Changed in Living Memory (History in Living Memory), Clare Lewis (Raintree, 2016)

See Inside Ships (Usborne See Inside), Conrad Mason (Usborne Publishing Ltd, 2010)

True or False? Transport, Dan Nunn (Raintree, 2014)

Websites

www.dkfindout.com/uk/search/transport/
Learn about the different types of transport in the UK.

http://www.bbc.co.uk/schools/primaryhistory/ancient_greeks/sea_and_ships/
Discover the types of ships in Ancient Greece.

Comprehension questions

1. What parts help ships to move through the water?

2. Why are ships good at transporting items?

3. Use another book or a website to learn about boats. How are ships different from boats? How are they similar?

Index